Peace over People

Ishika Raj

pencil

ISBN 978-93-5610-984-1

Published in India 2022 by Pencil

A brand of
One Point Six Technologies Pvt. Ltd.
123, Building J2, Shram Seva Premises,
Wadala Truck Terminal, Wadala (E)
Mumbai 400037, Maharashtra, INDIA
E connect@thepencilapp.com
W www.thepencilapp.com

CONTENTS

1 Crush

Ria Richards was excited for her 1st day of school, to meet new people, make new friends, and be happier than she was in her previous school. As soon as she reached her school Stuyvesant High School which was within a walking distance from her home.

She was starstruck by the magnificent infrastructure of her high school as she reached her class with the help of her homeroom teacher everyone was staring at her so she introduced herself,

"Hello everyone, myself Ria Richards I am from New Jersey . I hope we all become friends", Ria.

Everyone welcomed her super early she made a friend Nina, she was a sweet talker and a lovely person. No sooner did the day start than she bumped into some of her fellow mates they touched her hair saying," Pretty cool mate, you are pretty." Ria just smiled and went to the changing room to change into her PT uniform. Everyone tried to be Ria's friend because she had good grades and a pretty face. Ria learned all this plot in her previous girl's school. It was pretty difficult to adjust with the boys after being in all girls school but Ria knew it wasn't that difficult after having seven male cousins.

During the piano lessons class, she sat beside the Andrew Simons, Mr.Crush of school. She didn't know who he was she just saw the vacant seat and helped herself. Andrew started the conversation with her,

"Hi.

Ria replied,

"Hi, when she looked at his hazel eyes she was lost in him then and there. "Are you new here Ms.?" She took a moment, looked in his eyes, and replied,

"Ria, Ria Richards well I am new here, and what about you Mr.?"

He raised his left brow, looked into her grey eyes, and replied "Andrew, Andrew Simons well I am not new here." Ria chuckles and continued practicing her piano and was thinking about Andrew who was just sitting beside her she was already missing his presence by thinking that the class may end soon. The Piano teacher Ms.Katie Patrecia came to her place and asked her if she would like to enroll herself in the Drama play which would take place next month. Ria replied,

"I am a dancer but I enjoy playing piano but it's just a hobby I am not a professional pianist." Ms.Katie replied firmly,

"If you enjoy playing the piano ust try once", Ria nodded her head and agreed. Andrew said "Congratulations Partner," in confusion Ria asked,

"What?" He said, "you will know."

Ria rushed back to her classroom and asked Nina about Andrew and her response was "Don't you dare fall for him", which was super late. Nina asked Ria, "Already my friend?", Ria was processing her answer but her brain cells were numb and Nina's group of friends arrived Tyler the

tallest guy with a sarcastic aura, Gyaan with a turban and chubby face, Samuel and Ayden both good looking with a charming personality. Everyone was good to her and she knew she would have lovely two years with them.
But Ria's mind was just struck by the little conversation between her and Andrew. On her way back home Tyler accompanied her as his house was on the way to Ria's place. She saw Andrew walking ahead of them drinking soda and headphones plugged, his semi-curly black hair fluttering on his pale skin and his broad shoulders were making Ria hypnotize, he was as handsome as her dream boy she dreamt about every night. Tyler interrupted her thoughts by asking "do you live here"? Ria replied "yes, is something wrong?", Tyler said, "Andrew lives in your opposite apartment". She was all confused, happy, and nervous.

After the exhausting first day of new high school, Ria came straight to her room where she found no one just silence, and Mr.Cuddles, her dog barking. Ria lost his dad when she was just a baby, so she lived with her mother who was always busy with her job, and her dog Mr.Cuddles. They recently moved to New York City because of her mother's promotion, eventually, she was happy of moving to another city with strangers and New York City is popular for being the busiest place.

Weekend with Ria's amazing new friends Nina, Tyler, Gyaan, Samuel, and Ayden. Everyone was sweet and amusing towards Ria they shared their everyday family drama and some not funny jokes, they were down to earth and the fact that she was new didn't bother them, they didn't throw any tantrums. She felt comfortable and happy around them.

Ria was never excited about going to school earlier but the fact that she would get to see Andrew in her new school made her awake the entire night not that she didn't watch him all night by turning off her lights while sitting on her balcony's swing, she could only see was his curtains still she stared at it thinking how would his room look like, wondering about his smell and mesmerizing her thoughts by thinking about his hazel eyes. Early morning she groomed herself with a bow hairpin and the pleasant scent of cotton candy. She didn't want to let Andrew know that she lives opposite his apartment thinking maybe he wouldn't like it and take her for some of his lover girls as Nina recommended her to do so. As soon as she reached her classroom she heard some rumors of Tyler and Gyaan dating which made her happy and worried for them. Few girls came to her asking for the truth as Ria was a very good friend of Tyler but she realized he don't trust her yet and would not share a secret. Ria didn't wish to listen to anything so she left towards the art room, on the way she saw Andrew he also came towards her and said,

"Hi", she looked into his eyes and said,

"Hi" with a sad yet excited tone. Andrew gently asked her, "wanna listen to some music"? she smiled back and took his one earphone they were close enough for Ria to smell his scent it was chocolaty and he interrupted," it's my favorite song the night we met by Lord Huron". She noticed his ear piercing, and his toned arms, and was ashamed of her height as he was 6ft 2inch and she was just 5ft 2inch.

Bell rang so they left for the class together, while everyone was consoling Tyler and Gyaan or gossiping about them she was with Andrew which made her friends mad. She smiled and sat beside Andrew because Nina was sitting with Tyler. Andrew looked into her eyes and said "everything will be alright."Even though Tyler and Gyaan were facing issues Ria was sad as she was also trapped in some rumors in her previous school, saying she was a two-timing girl and at that difficult time, she had lost her two best friends Nadia and Julie because their respective boyfriends were treating them like trash and she suggested them to break up, instead of breaking up that toxic relationship they broke off their friendship with Ria. As soon as the English language class ended Ria went to Nina and asked what was wrong Ayden grabbed her hand and took her to the side and said, "Gyaan and Tyler have been dating for a year now but they never came out but Tyler is bi and Gyaan is gay and he was jealous watching you and Tyler spending time giggling and laughing so he uploaded cozy pics with Tyler without asking him and so stay quiet until everything is calmed down." Ria sighed and replied," I am sorry". Ayden felt bad for her so he said," We all love you Ria we know you are a nice person it's just the wrong time", Ria smiled, and as the school dismissed Tyler was waiting for her a and she was shocked yet happy so she asked him, "wanna share secrets"?

Tyler truly loved Gyaan as she could know by his words and those looks he carried when he was with him. Tyler and Gyaan apologized to Ria and thanked her as they came out. They both reconciled and they were back to being the old them. She wanted to thank Andrew for being there for her but she couldn't, Tyler knew Ria was head over heels for Andrew and so he said,

"Even if nothing feels appealing but his presence does then that's love".

2 Celebrations

Last night was again the same
bit of a pale still in denial
was it you again?
It's scarier and I am scared
and if Isay I have fallen for you
will you be in pain?
You fell for this girl
just before I realized my feelings
was this our gain?
Should I let go of you and our dreams
can we even call it ours these thoughts
run through my vein.

This is exactly how Ria felt after Andrew showed up with his girlfriend Sarah at the Fresher's party and the party was more like a partition for her.
After a huge ruckus of Tyler Nash and Gyaan Singh dating, there was a welcome party in which everyone needed a partner. Tyler and Gyaan were going together whereas Nina Gray wished to go with Samuel Sanchez, Ayden Gates and Ria Richards were left out but she wished to go with Andrew of course. She didn't tell anyone that she had a crush on Andrew except for his online best friend Theo, he had a great sense of humor and always hoped the best for Ria they shared their opinions, views,

and secrets their bond was growing over a year now. Theo Bush suggested to Ria, "ask Andrew out for the party", little did he know it was a mistake. The day before the party while practicing piano Andrew looked into Ria's eyes and said, "Hi, do you mind if I ask you a question?", Ria stared at him and replied, "Hi, you may." Andrew asked her," Did you shift to Galaxy apartment last month?" Ria lost words to speak and replied," were you stalking me?" Andrew glared at her, looked at Ria's wristwatch, and replied," not you but your dog". Ria sighed and said, "yeah my house is nearby". Andrew asked, "will you"? and was interrupted by a girl named Sarah, Andrew was introducing her and Sarah again interrupted and said, "can you excuse us for a moment, by the way, I am Sarah Andrew's girlfriend". Ria as use well smiled and left the art room.

Ria didn't have a partner so she decided to go alone, Theo suggested to her, "Why don't you ask Ayden?" Ria firmly denied it as she was just friends with her and didn't feel like going with him even though he was nice to her, she knew he had feelings for her, but she didn't want to give him any hopes. While the party was going on everyone was dancing with their partner and then Samuel came toward Ria and asked if she had like to go with Ayden while Ria was all confused, Steve called for her and asked if she had like to go with him so Ria said, "yes". Ria was all heartbroken by the fact of Sarah is Andrew's girlfriend and she was resenting herself as her friends were doing because she chose Steve over Ayden but for Ria, it wasn't about her feelings it was about the peace, she chose peace over people. Tyler and Nina came to her after the dance and asked what was all that as they were the closest to her she was hurt by that question and replied," Andrew was with his girlfriend so I didn't have the chance nor the luxury of going with whomever I wish to. I didn't want to go with Ayden as I knew his feeling and it would be a shame if he gets to know that he was just an option to me, and it's obvious that I am the bad person here." Nina said," forget the rest and do what you want like I did with going with Samuel even though we were a past but I still love him". Ria was just broken with what happened at the party so she just decided to leave when Andrew stopped her and said, "Hi, can we talk?" "Hi, yeah", she said. "Are you a thing with Steve?", he asked. "Why does it concern you in any way"? she asked in a brutal tone "Sarah is my

cousin, nobody knows about this she just wanted to make her boyfriend jealous", he replied. "I don't even know Steve's last name", she said.

They both went home back together, after all that party wasn't that bad for Ria. But she still wasn't ready to face Ayden, but their friendship meant a lot to her.

After all the drama at the party, Ria explained everything to Theo over text saying, "Ayden was angry and sad because of me so he simply ignored me, I felt guilty and thought of apologizing little did I know Ayden would already start dating Bella. I am happy for Ayden moving on, but seeing him hurt by me makes my heart hurt". Theo being a responsible friend advised, "but I still hope you can fix your 'friendship' it's beyond the distance between you and Ayden, there's none to blame listen to what your heart is speaking".

After a week Ria and Andrew were practicing piano together as they were partners and the song they chose was 'fur realize they were the show openers. Andrew in a soft

tone said,
"Hi, you smell nice.
"Hi, thanks it's sweet like candy by Ariana Grande", she replied. Andrew looked at her with those tender eyes every time she called him by his last name Simons. He loved the way she would look into his eyes and answer him. He wanted more every day and the fact that they are neighbors and our partner's in the musical play excited him in every way. During their practice hours, Ria's hair flipped on Andrew's face which he didn't mind, while he was lost in her thoughts Ria meddled in and asked him," Hi, Simon can you help me with this tune?" Andrew grabbed her fingers and played the piano with his hand on top of hers Ria was shocked while her heart fluttered, with butterflies in her stomach, with a spark in her eyes and unknowingly she had raised her expectations. "This is how you play it, if you find any difficulty make sure to ask, and are you taking your dog out today?" he said. "Thank's, yeah I will. Do you wanna join? I guess you like Mr. Cuddles?" she asked. He immediately replied, "cool, meet u and Mr. Cuddles at 7 near the fountain." They spent a lot of time talking about their interests and how their opinions mattered to each other, Ria's love for him was increasing in every possible way, but Andrew wasn't expecting Ria to be like other girls who confess to him every other day.

Nina and Ria were busy preparing for exams which were starting the next day of the drama play. Nina asked Ria if they could take a break, and said with nervousness," I and Samuel are back together", which Ria thought wasn't a good idea as she felt nostalgic. When she gave 'Swayer' her ex-boyfriend a second chance which she didn't regret nor did she enjoy, he was a great friend but a miserable boyfriend Ria still hoped they could start over but her high hopes were ruined by Swayer's countless mistakes. So she wished the best for Nina and said," I wish you all the happiness but if you feel unhappy anytime just break it of its better than suffering". As she had already experienced the worst heartbreak. Ever since Tyler and Gyaan came out they were making everybody uncomfortable by being Lovey Dovey yet they were an adorable couple. Tyler always helped Ria by giving her ideas to attract Andrew which she didn't require because Andrew was already staring at her every second she was in front of her. Andrew had a friend circle of a bunch of weirdos, Marco and Rowan were those pair of weirdos who made unnecessary judgments about teachers and fellow mates. The people Ria disliked the most, were people who judge them on their family status, clothes, and amount of money they waste in a club Marco and Rowan suited this introduction. Even though Ria adored Andrew she couldn't neglect his circle. During the practices, she came closer to Andrew and got to know him and he was exactly the way she thought he would be, intelligent and intellectual. The girly girl gang hated her for being close to Andrew which hardly mattered to her until Jenny questioned Ria on her relationship with Andrew and she replied with a frown, "your mom".

Ria knew being sweet to those people who bother her unnecessarily and bad mouth her are the worst also her mother had taught her to do as they do to her. Having a single parent was always tough she didn't even know what a father is but it was tougher for her mother who was criticized for being a widow and a workaholic who didn't look after her daughter but the truth was she did her best and Ria loved her mother and worshipped her presence.

3 Secret's

Finally, the day arrived. Nina was the host followed by Ayden and Samuel they were performing an act from the play Charlie Chaplin. Tyler decided to just click pictures and enjoy the play while Gyaan was playing the drums. Ria was nervous about her performance so Andrew grabbed her pinky finger and took her to the green room and said
"Hi, I am here for you so leave everything to me, will you?"Ria smirked and answered back
"Hi, but how long?" Andrew raised his brow came closer to her, looked into her deep grey eyes, and replied with a smile," the longer you can put up with". Both giggles.

Steve scrambled into the green room, saw Andrew and Ria close, and came to Ria yelled at her saying, "Well reason for rejecting me was your crush as per you. Is it Andrew? Your crush? Then Let me tell you we are brothers and he won't date you if I say so isn't it mate?" Andrew interrupted before any more rumors left the room," we are just partners in the play, we aren't anything besides that". Ria gulped she never felt this low about herself, Jenny stood there giggling after hearing all this. Ayden rushed in and glared at Andrew and Steve and said, "a bunch of pathetic losers, Ria let's go." Ria was feeling miserable but she was the show opener so she was preparing herself to go on stage and Ayden said," You can do it, we all will cheer for you, go ahead and nail it." Ria gave him a side hug and went up on stage where she had to tolerate Andrew's presence, her feelings for him were chapped by Andrew himself. They nailed the show and Ria ran into the washroom Andrew followed her and kept saying," I didn't mean it". Ayden sent Tyler to look after Ria explaining what happened earlier and Tyler in anger asked Andrew," Either you apologize or fuck off, Ria deserves better than you."

Ria's desire of being loved by Andrew, and all her sweet dreams became an unreal ugly truth for her. She felt that similar heartbreak again and questioned herself, "Do I don't deserve love?" Andrew called her several times and stood on his balcony looking for her but he gained no response so he went to her house and her homemaker opened the door and offered him water while she called Ria and Andrew saw a notepad lying on the corner of the room he picked up and tucked it inside his jacket. Ria came out and said, "Hi", as if nothing ever happened, he replied," Are you going out with Ayden?" "Why the fuck does that concern you in any way?" she replied in anger. He came close to her, wiped her tears, and said," I should know about you, don't I deserve to know at least this much?" "Are you leaving or should I kick you out"?she said. He locked the room and said, "we need to clear the misinterpretations, or even better we could do something about this situation." "No, I would pass I don't want to have any conversation," Ria replied. "Cool", Andrew said and moved towards the couch where Ria was sitting and looked into her eyes, and asked " May I?" Ria always dreamt about this situation and Mr. Cuddles barked and interrupted their eye contact. Andrew again said, "It's the first time I have," Ria gave him a peck on his lips. Andrew felt her warm small lips which he wanted to kiss for the longest time Andrew grabbed her face and leaned her onto the cushion and came closer to her lips and kissed her they could hear each other's heartbeat. Every time Ria flipped her hair back Andrew wanted to kiss her neck mole so before kissing her neck he whispered, " Was this a yes? Will you go out with me? I didn't want to make you uncomfortable so I disagreed when Steve asked me about us I thought you wouldn't like it". Ria said, " Simon" Andrew didn't let her finish the sentence and kissed her again and this time it was more passionate he played with her earlobe and Ria touched and fueled his semi-curly hair as he appeared more handsome to deal with.

Their bond changed overnight all the mixed feelings she was going through all at once were unbearable so she called Theo and told him what happened he was

Another series of problems in Ria's life, she didn't know if she was dating Andrew or not after such a passionate kiss she still needed a confession but the exams were on the head instead of Andrew's lesson she was supposed to study Accountancy lessons.

"I remember I cried the most last night not because I got bad grades nor did a guy break my heart but because the companions did, I trusted those who bad-mouthed me, and not only did they spread baseless rumors but also spoke extremely ill about me. But I am glad and grateful for being rich as in having a house to call home, living a wealthy and healthy lifestyle, and having a loving Mumma with my caring Grandpa for whom I am dearest. But now I am also grateful for having such wonderful kind-hearted friends and of course, Andrew whose presence delights my heart and mind."

As Theo suggested giving hints would be the best way to Andrew's heart so I unfollowed him and followed him back on Instagram which didn't make any difference then next step was stalking him in school which he didn't even bother and the final step was to ask him for the dance but he had already chosen Sarah to be her partner so I just asked him for a picture and came back home all sad. Even though we lived nearby I was hardly able to see him." and the notepad ended. After Andrew read her notepad which comprised her secrets and the poems she wrote for him, his love, respect, and admiration for Ria increased. Early morning Tyler came to pick her up where he saw Andrew already waiting for her he understood Andrew's facial expression that they have reconcile and so he waited at a distance and allowed them to proceed. "Hi, are you prepared for the exam.?" Andrew asked. "Hi, well I don't know about the exam but my head hurts," she replied. "All you did was dance all night on indie pop music, I didn't try to see it was just that your music was loud and the curtains of your room were transparent". Andrew said. Ria was embarrassed yet she was blushing.

After their exam, Tyler came to Ria and said he would go back home with Samuel and winked at her, and said," I need all the details super soon". Ria blushed and replied," after you lover boy." Andrew came running to her and asked, "is your head paining, did you write well? It's okay even if it wasn't, let me carry your bag for you. Ria smiled and said," Were you always this handsome?" They both smiled at each other and went back home. Ria didn't know what Andrew was thinking about the thing going on between them nor did she want to get hurt so she didn't try to ask him. Ayden called her up and asked her to meet up in the evening which she thought she should tell Andrew but why should she be asking him was the question? Everything was messed up Ria needed clarities so she could give statements to those people who bad mouth them. So she called up Andrew and he asked her to come over. Ria came all dressed up as she also had to go to meet Ayden. Andrew was struck by seeing her so he took a pause and said, "were you always this pretty, or is it just my eyes"? Ria replied, " like Andrew like Ria". Andrew offered her coffee which she denied saying she had to meet someone. Andrew in a confused tone asked, "I am hurt, you didn't dress up for me?" Ria saw her notepad on the window slab, and in anger, she asked " What is this doing here? Did you read it? Andrew being her crush was one of Ria's deepest secrets and her biggest fears, her feelings and the dark emotions she faced were all stolen from her. Andrew nervously replied," It's okay I don't judge you. Ria had never been this angrier, especially with someone she loved this much, "It's better if we act like strangers." Andrew interrupted and said, "after all that we have?" "It was a mistake for me and my words were secret for a reason and you stole my diary?" she yelled at him and left saying this.

Ria realized falling in love, living that love, and sharing love with your partners isn't easy at all. She was sad, she wanted Andrew to be with her but not with pity but with love.

4 Summer

After the exams, Samuel planned a celebration in his backyard. Ria wasn't planning on going as she canceled her meetup last minute with Ayden saying she wasn't feeling well. Andrew couldn't reach Ria at the moment as she turned her phone off and went to the dance academy with her new friend Sarah.

Sarah Simons and Ria Richards practiced dance together they majored in contemporary form. Sarah knew about Ria's feelings towards Andrew and so she often teased her, earlier when Ria didn't know Andrew and Sarah were cousins she decided to let go of her feelings because Sarah was sweet to her, and she didn't want to lose a loving friend as Sarah was a kind-hearted person with a pleasing smile on her face. She was relieved to know that they were cousins. While practicing Ria made several mistakes and her beautiful performance was ruined by the frown on her face, Sarah and Ms. Dee tried asking her but Ria didn't respond. Sarah was concerned so she called up her brother and asked him to come to take her home. Andrew came to pick Ria and he said," I am sorry for making you feel this way I won't give any excuse I knew I made a huge mistake. Out of curiosity, I read your secret I am ashamed of myself. Can you at least give me another chance?" Ria ignored him and went inside her apartment complex and

Andrew shouted, "I am sorry, I will wait for you at the party".Ria felt betrayed and wasn't ready to face the situation.

On the other hand, Nina Gates was questioning herself if she made an indecisive decision for giving Samuel Sanchez a second chance as he wasn't expressing his thoughts or reciprocating feelings. Nina thought about Ria's advice and decided to speak to Samuel about it.

Ria was getting dressed up for the party when Gyaan called her and said," All you do is look pretty and act victim after playing with two guys' hearts. Tyler is foolish and has worn a blindfold when it's about you but let me tell you your poor girl mask will be thrown once I tell them what you were like in your previous school." As in her previous school, she was accused of being a two-timing girl. Ria smirked and replied," Are you concerned or jealous Gyaan, I thought you disliked me but you are an unloyal pet who hates me for being better than you. You say you love Tyler and you don't even trust him. Go spread whatever you wish I know what kind of person I am and I don't owe any explanation." Ria hung up on him and left for the party. As soon as she reached there Tyler came to her and said," I didn't know you and Andrew were dating," Ria replied, "Are we?" Tyler said, "Steve and Andrew argued, and Andrew said you are his girl." Ria rushed to find Ayden she knew he would be upset about the situation but fortunately, he was busy making out with Bella across the dining area. Andrew came to her closer and closer, looked Into her eyes, and said, "Hi, can we please have a fresh start with just you and me, I have no room for misunderstandings and secrets." Ria had a lot on her mind, but Andrew was the only person who made her heart flutter and happy so she whispered," depends on your performance". Andrew blushed and said, "I am all yours, my girl". Both hugged each other and enjoyed the party with others. Gyaan and Tyler were in an argument, Samuel tried to keep them calm but it didn't help. Whereas Nina was mad at Samuel for not giving her any attention. Samuel was continuously talking to Sarah about the upcoming dance event which made the situation even worse.

The evening wasn't good for a few but was warm and cozy for the love birds. Ayden and Bella were having a romantic evening. Whereas Ria was staring at Andrew the entire evening thinking, "why is he this tall? How is his voice seductive? Even his piercing enhances his jawline and every time he puts his fingers around my waist it tickles me and gives me butterflies." The evening's atmosphere was just as Theo commented on Ria's picture last night, "<3 is in the air". staring at Andrew the entire evening thinking, "why is he this tall? How is his voice seductive? Even his piercing enhances his jawline, and every time he puts his fingers around my waist it tickles me and gives me butterflies." The evening's atmosphere was just as Theo commented on Ria's picture last night,
"<3 is in the air".

Ayden Gates and Steve Marz had a huge crush on Ria and even though they tried they couldn't forget her. They knew Andrew and Ria are dating but still couldn't accept the reality. Whereas Gyaan made a huge conflict between all five of them, he provoked Ayden to separate Ria and Andrew. Tyler and Gyaan broke up at the party while

Samuel and Nina were struggling with themselves. Ayden and Steve disliked each other's presence.
Summer vacation began and Ria wrote this on her notepad as she was feeling the best she could at the moment as she was having Andrew by her side.

"Summer morning with watermelon in my bowl
with sweat all over my collar bone
kid's hooting and playing with the ball
relatively warm from the veranda to watch wanted an ice cream cone.
Trees were still,a sudden breeze
as wind chimes and curtains blew,
brought us relief saw some dancing bees
observing those little moments was charming in brief."

Ever since the vacation started Andrew and Ria came over to their respective balcony and chatted over the phone with each other. They took Mr. Cuddles out in the evening, and they laughed and ate while holding each other's hand. Nina sent her an emergency text that she was coming over, Ria was concerned for her and asked, "Hey, what's wrong? Are you alright?" Nina replied," I received a picture of Samuel and Sarah making out near the Bookswoon Library." Ria felt nostalgic as she had already been through this situation when her ex-boyfriend Swayer and her ex-best friend Isabella cheated on her. "Ria hugged Nina as she busted out in tears. But Ria didn't fall for the picture and required major proof to confront Samuel so she made a plan with Nina. Ria called Samuel to the mid-street saying Nina was injured so he came running in a few minutes, Nina wasn't there and Ria was standing alone. "

This isn't a joke, is it?" Samuel asked. "If you care so much about Nina why don't you tell her,' he interrupted Ria and said, "I do care for Nina but as a friend, I don't have feelings for her in that way anymore." The worst part of his confession was Nina was listening to all this through the Bluetooth headset. Ria showed him the picture of him kissing Sarah, he was embarrassed and Nina came there and grabbed Ria's hand and ran away.
Ria straight away went to Andrew's home and explained to him that Samuel cheated on both Sarah and Nina, Andrew calmed himself and sent Ria to look after Nina, and he went to Sarah. Ria realized that the picture sent to Nina was by an unknown number so she emailed the number to her cousin Harry who worked in a network agency. The vacations she dreamt of were ruined it was as worst as it could be. When she came back home after making Nina feel better she was tired and needed to sleep, on the stairs, Andrew was waiting for her he pulled her into the lift and whispered, " leave it to me, my girl." He removed her hair from her face and hugged her which Ria required the most at the moment. As soon as she came back home her cousin Harry emailed her saying it was under Singh's name. Ria never thought Gyaan Singh would do such a thing, if he would have been a true friend he would have gone to Nina and explained the scenario which he made worse. Ria called Tyler and informed him immediately, Tyler was sad as he never expected Gyaan to harm the feelings of their mates.

Being a teenager, handling any relationship and friendship isn't a burden but a wonderful experience that many people don't get. But if you have someone you love and they love you back respecting their time, and maintaining loyalty is the least one could do which was left for Gyaan, Samuel, Ayden, and Steve to learn.

5 Confessions

Ria's Mumma took her to her grandpa to spend some family time for a few days. Ria needed this break to come back stronger also it made her feel refreshed and happy. Whereas Andrew was taking care of his grandparents, he had a big loving family with responsible parents and an elder brother who pampered him like a baby. They were enjoying their summer.

"What did you wear"? Theo asked
"Theo you tell me what's the point of wearing a mini skirt if he is not gonna slip his hands between my thighs and finger me with his toned veined hands and smirk at me while I struggle to contain my moans. Am I not attractive enough?"
Ria replied in frustration.
While their extremely steamy discussion, Theo was thinking about someone else. Theo had a crush on Tyler as they spend a lot of time together because of Ria, but he knew about the situation of Gyaan going around and didn't want to make Ria concerned so he kept it a secret. After returning home from her vacation, Andrew wasn't paying attention to Ria in a romantic way and she felt under-confident about herself. But there were more things to worry about as in Gyaan and his determination of breaking their group and it was divided into three each. Nina was on

a vacation with her elder sister for a therapy session. She had decided to break Samuel's nose once she returns stronger, Sarah had blocked Samuel and decided to confront him when school reopens in front of Nina. Tyler was trying to move on and Theo was helping him out by jamming together on indie pop music and working out together.

Andrew never confessed his actual feelings for Ria, which he regretted as he already knew how Ria felt about him. He was confused about how to tell her, so he was acting pretty distant from her for the past few days also his ex-girlfriend Emily was continuously reaching out to him. He wanted to have a long conversation with Ria so he called her up to his place. As soon as she reached his place he took her to his bedroom which Ria always dreamed of she went to his balcony and saw the view of her room from there. His room was filled with pictures of different places he wanted to travel to, he had many novels and a Casio of course he loved playing piano like he loved playing football. Ria hugged Andrew for bringing her to his room, her smile made Andrew's day and he thought if just his presence could make her happy he wanted to give her all he had. Andrew hugged Ria back tightly and whispered," I wanted to talk to you", Ria stepped back and said, "Oh yeah, go ahead". Andrew pulled her back, held her waist, looked into her eyes, and said, "I love the way you look at me, how your pretty eyes stare at me, I often lose control over myself when you are in front of me just like now I always imagined this situation and Ria, trust me being this pretty could be an unbearable pain for my heart because every time I come closer to you your face becomes pink and I wish to make every part of you pink which I can't even see." Ria blushed and turned around. Andrew held her from the back and gave a peck on her neck and said," You are driving me crazy Ria, I like you." after a pause he turned her around and asked her," Why aren't you saying anything, are my feeling's burden to you?" she nodded and said," what took you so long and I like you more and more." Andrew said, "stop me If I cross the limits," he kissed her, and this time he used his tongue. Ria pushed him onto the couch, and Andrew pulled her and made her sit on his lap, she rubbed her hands on his abs, Andrew smirked, and said,"you are turning me on and it might be dangerous". "If that's the case, I can take it as long as it's you." Ria replied. Both chuckled and watched the sunset from his balcony.

While few were making love, and conditioning their bond, the not-so-reasonable group of people was planning on how to get rid of the unity and love they share.

Vacations were coming to an end and Bella broke up with Ayden as he still had feelings for Ria. Samuel wasn't responding to any texts or calls from anyone because he was regretting what he did to Nina and Sarah. Ayden's birthday party was on the last day of the vacation. Gyaan was feeling lonely without Tyler and he blamed Ria for his breakup, so he planned on calling Emily to Ayden's birthday party to create a scene between Ria and Andrew.

Ria didn't plan on going she knew if she were there with Andrew, Gyaan will draw Ayden's attention to them and it would ruin his day. Andrew planned for a movie date with Ria as his family went to attend a wedding. Tyler and Theo got closer and Ria knew they are a thing. Tyler and Theo were working out together, when Theo unbuttoned his shirt as he had showered in sweat, Tyler was busy staring at his abs and asked in nervousness," are you interested in playing?" Theo came closer to Tyler, looked into his eyes and smirked at him, and said "Well, I am more interested in what you are thinking." Tyler replied," are you trying to romance me?" Theo said, "working pretty well, isn't it?" Tyler moved backward and giggled saying "I was talking about Minecraft." Theo just gave a smile and said, "not today, I already have plans." Whereas Gyaan's plan was ruined because neither Ria nor Andrew showed up. Nina went to Samuel and had some drinks with him, Samuel took her to his car as she was already high after two drinks. Nina cried, yelled, and expressed everything she had gone through because of him. Nina stepped out of his car and bumped into Jacob, Ayden's brother. Jacob and Nina danced together at the party and they were drunk, she came closer to him but Jacob took her to Ayden and he dropped her home.

Ria groomed herself and when Andrew opened his door, the moment he saw her he said," you are catching my curiosity, my girl, instead of watching a movie I had like to explore you a little." It was Theo's idea and he suggested to Ria, "seduce him but don't get carried away." Ria went inside smiling and took off her shrug while Andrew turned on the movie, 'My Fake Boyfriend'. They were enjoying the movie when Ria came closer and sat beside him she skimmed his pants and got the air conditioner controller beside Andrew. She went to his kitchen to make some coffee and acted like she can't reach the coffee mugs so she called for Andrew and while Andrew was taking out the mugs she turned around and came closer to his lips and whispered," thanks". Andrew was also playing along but couldn't take it anymore," while Ria was drinking coffee he said," Fuck it", grabbed her waist lifted her, and placed her on top of him, "whatever your plan is, it's working". Ria flipped her hair back, unbuttoned his shirt, and licked his lips while he bites her neck, ria moaned, and Andrew pushed her onto the couch, " do you like it?" He was licking her thighs and she was moaning, "you don't like it?" He pressed Ria's breast and whispered, "should I stop"? Ria was perceiving the pleasure she wished for and was moaning when he just licked her breasts, she said," stop, we need to stop, someone is calling you for so long." The awkwardness was roaming in the air but when Ria saw his phone she lost her cool it had ten unread texts from Emily and a few missed calls. "Aren't you going to explain yourself?" Ria questioned in a frustrated tone. "As you see, she is after me because she got dumped by her boyfriend, but I didn't even dare to look at her after all I am with the national fairy 'The Ria Richards," Andrew replied. Ria busted into laugh and replied," How cliche, don't you dare say that again." They both smiled at each other and went out to take a stroll.

While love was reaching its door some truths and lies were also waiting downstairs. Thus, few bonds were fading in the air and new bonds were cherishing in waves.

6 Roller Coaster

Summer break was officially over, and the drama parade of every third person began in school. It was tiring and bothersome for everyone except for the love birds. While Tyler was busy missing Theo, Nina was recalling yesterday's memories, and Ayden was sad that their friends are no longer as close as they were earlier. While Gyaan was working on his plan, he included Marco and Rowan in breaking Andrew and Ria.

Emily regretted breaking up with Andrew so she called him over but she didn't get any response. Andrew's friends were envious of him as Andrew was a pro athlete, with good grades and a charming personality, he could woo a girl just by his looks, and he now had Ria 'the ideal girl'. Marco and Rowan planned on destroying Andrew, they took him to the changing room and had a conversation about how is Ria in bed. Andrew found this question very personal and replied, "aren't you both getting personal and stop talking absurd about us", the moment he said this Emily entered the boys changing room. Rowan and Marco left them alone and went back to the class and stood beside Ria as if they didn't see her and talked about how Emily came into the boys changing room to have a conversation with Andrew. Ria hurried in a panic to the changing room and after what she saw and heard she never wanted to go back to school.

Ria was already pissed since last night because of her mother's absence, everybody thought she smiled because she was happy but she was just hiding her sadness. While growing up she didn't know what a family meant, she celebrated her birthdays alone, she slept alone even when she was hurt or ill, and nobody was there by her side but she never complained. Just her mother's presence made her happy, she knew her mother suffered more but she couldn't bear eating alone as she lost 10kgs which made her severely ill after spending a few months in hospital her mother got her Mr.Cuddles, he became her best buddy she shared her thoughts, complained about how everybody annoys her and she adored him like he was his younger sibling. However, last night made history for the mother and daughter as they never fought before, Ria told her mother about her dating Andrew which made her mum concerned and angry. Her mother knew how worse her first heartbreak was and she didn't want to see her suffer more so she said," before he ends this, it's better if you go ahead and end this first, he will make you suffer." Ria cried out and said," He isn't like you, he won't leave me when I need him the most." After the argument, Ria slammed the door and locked herself in, they both equally felt bad for yelling at each other. Ria went to her homeroom teacher and asked for a leave saying she was on her menstrual cycle because of which her abdomen pains. The moment she was packing her bag to leave she saw everyone was gawking at her, Nina and Tyler took her to the corner and showed her the cozy pictures of her and Andrew which were photoshopped and blurred Andrew's face. It was uploaded by an unknown username on the school's social networking page. Ria was in shock and tears when Andrew came toward her she said, "Jerk" and left in anger. Ria's mother was called to the school and had to hear some extremely bad rumors about her going around. The school faculty members were better than Mrs.Richards thought they believed in Ria and took down the pictures from their official page but asked her to stay home unless the matter cooled down which she denied and said," My daughter is not to blame here and she will come to school no matter what, some students have tried to ruin my daughter's character with baseless rumors, you'll better not force me to take legal action against the school's negligence and grab this last chance to find the mysterious student who is behind it." Whereas Ria on the other end was breaking into pieces, Tyler, Theo, and Nina came over to look after her when her mother wasn't home. Mrs.Richards worked as a Supervisor in the Central Hospital of New Citix, so when she came back home Ria hugged her mother and said, "I am sorry mum, I am ashamed of myself".

They hugged each other and reconciled.

I would have to tell you, you have bewitched me, body and soul, and I love... I love... I love you.I never wish to be parted from you from this day on", Mr. Darcy to Ms. Elizabeth Bennet. Ria and Nina sobbed while watching the movie.

Andrew kept his balcony door closed and didn't step out of his room. He was as miserable as Ria. The fact that his past with Emily was a wonderful experience but it was past and now he only wanted to fix things between Ria and him. He was hurt that Ria didn't even give him a chance to prove his point nor did she trust him and why would she after what she saw and heard. But from Andrew's point, it was all a planned trap in which she was caught. But was she caught?Nina couldn't remember anything from the party so she asked Ayden about what happened, he said," you were all over Jacob Gates and he is madly in love with you I guess, he keeps asking me every other day that you asked about him or not." Nina blushed and replied," is it so"? "So is the response mutual?" Nina replied and said, "Can I come over and meet Jacob". "Of course, you can just call me before you come.", Ayden replied. A relationship was the last thing on Tyler's mind he just wanted Theo to be his friend and his peace and rest everything would fall in place if it's meant to be. Theo was also not sure about his feelings as he had never dated a guy before. Whereas Samuel was busy working on himself to make himself presentable to Sarah and to have a fresh start, sadly Sarah ignored him or gave him looks every time he showed up but Samuel didn't give up. Gyaan, Marco, and Rowan were scared of getting got as the teachers were after the mysterious illegal student so they planned not to show up at school.

Ria and Andrew ignored each other in school. Andrew withdrew himself from the Piano club so that Ria doesn't feel uncomfortable, he spent most of the time playing and also avoided any conversation with Marco and Rowan. Whoever circulated any sort of opinion about Ria, Andrew started getting offensive and harsh. Ayden thought it was the perfect time for him to have a good impression on Ria so she went to her place and sat beside him saying, " Hey, how are you doing, I mean I know things aren't going well I told you he wasn't the right guy for you." "So who's the right guy? You? Who assumes to be a casanova and can play with any girl's feelings. Is feelings a joke to you? Just get lost and never look me in the eye." Ria humiliated him in front of his fellow mates. Everyone who thought Ria was sad and easygoing was in shock. After which Ria wrote a note to Andrew which said,

Average answer for the reasons you ask,
you know, stop pretending, and continue your task.
It will be okay if you abandon your annoying thought,
it makes me the wrong person, and that's exactly what I don't want.
Done with your split behavior so takeoff your ideal mask,
my shoulders are burdened with alone overtask.
Planned our ways together but you are harder than I thought,
begging for happiness is not what I want.

She gave this note to Tyler and he passed it to Andrew, he responded to it by saying,

Burnt the pictures we had, dropped the ash on my way back but I will cherish the memories we amassed, all your gifts were thrown in that sack.
I had those qualities those guys lack, good for nothing? I am loaded with cash. You thought I must be crack,since you left I am having a grand bash.
Needless your tears and regards,probably it felt to smash me so hard you are the queen I pulled while playing

cards,it's not the end, I love you but my heart has left bombard.

The poetic wars ended and their words for each other triggered them. Ria and Andrew missed each other but couldn't beat the reality and kept their distance. The presence of each other was torturing for the students but it wasn't enough yet there was more to come.

After those tough nights and days, Andrew didn't cry nor did anything about it. He pretended as if nothing happened and kept his cool. While others were just vibing and spilling some more baseless rumors.

7 Betrayal

Deep down everyone knows it's inevitable, that one day the one you trust and love the most will undoubtedly break you or vice versa. Living the moment and rejoicing in the memories were the only possible ways for one's happiness.

Ria had Pistanthrophobia she knew everyone would leave her one or the other day but unknowingly she got engaged in his eyes and believed in everything he conveyed, choosing peace for herself is the least she could do to show her love for herself. Ria visited her grandpa and during their conversation, he asked her a question, "Dear is there someone who would look after you if your mum and I aren't there?" Ria busted into tears and hugged her grandpa, her voice was breaking but she said," It's just you and mum, grandpa. Please don't leave me I can't bear the pain of loneliness it isn't easy for me." Ria knew how hard it was for her to even think of it, when Ria was in her junior year her grandpa pranked her he acted to lie down dead Ria cried and screamed as loud as she could his grandpa immediately hugged her and said, "My dear, I am completely fine." After that day Ria checked on him every minute, didn't leave his shadow, called him every day, and visited him every weekend when she moved to New York City.

While the PT period was going on Ayden stood beside Ria and said," have you heardthis, when the winds of change blow, some people build walls and others build windmills." "Well If you don't recall I can assure you I built a line between us in simple words it means to stop meddling in one's business, piss off." Ayden was angry and was about to yell at her when Andrew grabbed Ria's hand and ran over to the cellar of the school. Ria was continuously screeching at him but he didn't let go of her. Andrew pushed her to the wall and said, " what did he say? You aren't just giving up on us, are you? I will go nuts will you explain what's going on?" Ria pulled him closer and whispered," just forget the rest for the moment and kiss me." Andrew pulled her by her waist and replied," Not unless you explain to me what's going on." Ria kept her hands on his shoulder and gave a peck on his lips and said," have faith in me I am doing all this for us." I want to kiss you slowly with the lights on and the type of kiss which you could never put a price on but right now tell me everything why do we have to act like we aren't together anymore, tell me." Ria was staring at him so they proceeded making out in the dark when Tyler knocked," are you both down there, come back before things get suspicious." They went separately to the class. Andrew never had a friend who loved him even when he didn't love himself who would stick by his side even if things were worse, but after having Ria by his life glitter was shattered in his plain life. He respected and loved Ria's friends and how they took care of them in the bad times.

Yesterday Nina went to Ayden's and he sent her upstairs to Jacob's room, he was taking a shower and Ayden made the situation awkward yet intense he locked them inside. When Nina entered his room he saw his childhood pictures and trophies he won in the basketball tournament, and Jacob entered his room with his bathrobe on, he was shocked and asked Nina, "what are you doing here? Can you just wait outside while I change? Nina tried opening the door but couldn't so she replied, " I would like to but the door perhaps is locked." Jacob sighed and replied, "it's Ayden, that single moron". He offered Nina a seat and said," Finally, do you remember that night?" Nina explained," actually no." "So what do you want to prompt what happened that night?" Jacob replied. Nina was confused and Jacob kissed her and that's how they commenced, while Samuel, Ayden, and Steve were trying to move on. Tyler and Theo were confused about liking each other and they continued being confused.

Having genuine friends is such a blessing.No competition, no envy, no tittle-tattle, or any other negativity. Just good vibes, love, and happiness.

It was always there growing every day
but it came into notice while the relay
the struggles were delayed, the new world welcomed probably that wasn't the case,
it seemed more like a cage.
The beginning was bitter, but the chapter flips every day
defeating and conquering were the only way
it's ok that's what they said, none stood for myself
nevertheless, I will try my best.

When Ria came to New York City she wrote this to build her confidence little did she know this would help her in her toughest time.
So this is what exactly happened on the day Ria's picture went viral, Ayden overheard Gyaan, Emily, Marco, and Rowan making a plan to break their friendship and relationships so he went to Ria and explained their plan to her. Ria and Ayden plotted to let them think that they succeeded, to see their next move Andrew, Ayden, Theo, Tyler, Nina, and Ria were all included in the plan. That Day Ria already told Andrew about the highlights of their plan in brief and without answering his questions Ria just whispered to him," do as I say". Emily went and hugged him while Ria was hiding in the boys changing room, Andrew resisted and said," I am in love with Ria, so stop it now. Get a hold of yourself and this is my last conversation with you." Ria was in tears after all those phrases she was dying to hear but she had to keep her act together. Gyaan wanted to steal Ria's phone and send himself all the pictures she had with Andrew, so she left her phone unlocked on the table and allowed him to steal it herself but all the pictures were deleted. So they photoshopped some pictures from the web and uploaded them.Ria acted as if Andrew cheated on her which he didn't and when he came closer to her she yelled at him cried and said, "Jerk". Andrew was as confused as Ria's other friend. Ria didn't know that they would photoshop pictures and upload them on the school forum so she called her mother and explained how Gyaan has spread pictures, so her mother yanked at the school's image. Ria wanted to see how worse can someone do out of jealousy. Andrew was ashamed of being friends with Marco, Rowan,

and Emily. Ria fooled her mother to make her believe that she can endure the heartbreak and the betrayal and that she can live by herself all she needs is peace but Mrs.Richards knew Ria doesn't trust Andrew and she thinks being with him eternally is just her favorite incomplete wish.

Ria made things work as Gyaan planned, ignored Andrew, and made him write a breakup note. Yelled at Andrew and Ayden in front of everyone so that they believe they aren't friends anymore. They didn't even meet near their neighborhood nor did they talk to each other on their phone and Ria's friends came over to discuss the plan when her mother wasn't there, so her mother falls for the plan. Ria's mother was mad at her for lying and acting but at the same time, she was proud of her. She always thought she wasn't a good mother, and never taught her daughter anything. Ria herself became mature but after seeing Ria fight for her loved ones and showing true sides of people, she was feeling accomplished as a mother. Andrew wanted adventure and ever since he was with Ria he was amazed by her, every day seemed different and her love for him always excite him, he felt adventurous. "Simon, I told you this is how you make a panda with clay, we should take polaroid pictures more often, we should go to the mountains hiking with everyone, Simon are you listening?" Andrew was busy staring at her as he missed her and he realized even if he read her notepad yet there was a lot to discover her. He was still mad at himself for his stupidity in reading her notepad. While their breakup act Andrew realized how much Ria meant to him and he loved her, he didn't want to wait any longer and wanted to tell her how much she meant to him and how much he loved her.

The roller coaster ride was over.The hardships have prepared all of them for an extraordinary destin. Yet there was more to come.

8 Merry-Go-Round

"The person we need the most teaches us we need nobody." Living alone Ria had discovered no one would be there by her side forever.

"What did you wish for?" Andrew asked. "Just a peaceful life with a loving family." Ria sobbed. Every time she visited the church and spoke about her family her face became red and she got emotional. Andrew knew how she has endured being lonely and unhappy and he wanted to make sure she doesn't feel the misery again.

When the love birds were reuniting, the affection Nina was putting in for Jacob wasn't coming back with the same energy. Nina just started moving on but couldn't trust Jacob after what Samuel did to her. Nina saved Samuel's reputation by not saying her side of the story, but she knew she was strong enough to let go of him and leave a peaceful yet romantic life ahead, all she needed was time. Jacob and Nina knew each other for six years and they have been friends for five years, Nina always discovered him to be a gentleman and a handsome guy whereas Jacob always thought Nina to be a sweet and pretty girl, and he appreciated their friendship. He didn't have any dating experience nor did he have time for it, he was very focused on his sports, academics, and fulfilling their parent's expectations, unlike Ayden who was barely good in any way but was a loyal friend. Nina was waiting for Jacob to ask her out but he didn't, he didn't want any distraction so he kept a distance from her ever since they kissed in his room. Sarah liked Samuel so she wanted to forgive him and start over again but she couldn't as Andrew and Ria had strictly prohibited her to do so, she didn't want to regret so she took a chance and met Samuel. After an intense and serious conversation, Sarah decided to let go of him because she was concerned for herself. Samuel replied, " I chose you over Nina." Which made the situation worse, Sarah smiled and said," We were options, so let me choose this time, I shall choose my peace over you, nobody can play with me, even if I love them." Sarah left with her dignity with satisfaction. Tyler and Theo enjoyed being flirty with each other and spent their time playing games. Whereas Gyaan, Emily, Marco, and Rowan were in detention and the rest of them were enjoying their peaceful life.

Mrs.Richards wasn't much happy about the fact that Ria was dating Andrew but seeing her happy she accepted the reality and asked Andrew to look after her as he did the past few days. Andrew still couldn't understand a few things and had many questions to ask so he started as soon as they went for a stroll with Mr. Cuddles. "Why did you make me write those poems? Why did you ignore me even when we were at home it was unbearable?""To be in character Simon, it was difficult but now we know how it feels to be separated and how things became worse without any explanations," Ria replied. "Well that's true, we have gone through a lot so how about a chill Sunday with everyone at the amusement park? Andrew said. Ria got super excited and hugged him on the streets and said," I love you, you are the best." Andrew was shocked and happy he lifted her and said, "what? Do you love me???" Ria giggled and ran with Mr. Cuddles towards her home. Sarah, Nina, Ayden, Tyler, Theo, Andrew, and Ria were excited for the Sunday. They missed spending time jointly without any negative energy. Even though Ayden liked Ria he planned on staying just friends with her. Andrew disliked him but kept his cool for Ria's sake. Nina kept waiting for Jacob's acknowledgment. Andrew was busy thinking about Ria's 'I love you' while playing the piano. He joined his piano classes back after getting a huge lecture from Ms.Katie.

Theo planned to confront all the gossip and his secrets to Ria so he went to her and expressed how confused he has felt ever since he had feelings for Tyler, when Ria lived in New Jersey she never knew she could ever meet Theo from New York City but she shifted and met her generous and nicest buddy from past two years, she replied and comforted him," get honest with people about who you are, what you want, and how you expect to be treated. The standards may scare off people who aren't meant for you."

Every serene smile is hiding deep pain
and needs someone who can release pressure from the brain.
Eternal love, they say probably never stays,
destiny will be in our favor and they will envy us.
My heart hurts because of their measure
it takes time but heal's sooner or later.

Need your back in a blaze of glory
as in I hope together we cry and fly.

Ria wrote this in her notepad but wasn't over it yet and wanted to slam all four of them, early morning Ria reached school with her friends and waited for them in the corridor. As soon as they reached Ria asked Gyaan," how does it feel of getting trapped in your plan? Tyler jumped in and said," you still aren't guilty, are you? How could you do this? After you leaked our pictures, still leaked Ria's fake picture? Andrew in anger replied, " guilty, they? Betrayed me and made a joke about our friendship of five years. I am ashamed of myself for turning a blind eye to you Emily, Marco, and Rowan. I hope I never have to see your faces again." Ayden interrupted," Ria didn't break our friendship you did Gyaan, your insecurities did. Now suffer you all deserve it." Gyaan, Emily, Marco, and Rowan were sad and could not look them in their eyes so they faced downwards.

It had been a tough week for them, so before going to the Amusement Park Ria and Nina went on a shopping spree. Nina was still lost in Jacob's thoughts whereas Ayden was explaining and making Jacob realize that his happiness was in Nina," you can balance things, make it work brother a few earn the same love and efforts you give in from the opposite person. It's not a burden instead it's the love you can hold hand in hand emotionally, mentally, sexually, and spiritually." Jacob realized how he was letting go of Nina and hating himself every moment so he saw himself in the mirror and decided to confess to her tomorrow on the Ferris wheel. Nina didn't have any expectations but she knew that she liked Jacob. Theo didn't want to be another

Gyaan for Tyler he liked him but for staying by his side he decided to be his forever friend and Tyler felt the same way. Everyone was excited about their amusement park outing and later the guys planned for a barbecue for dinner. Tyler's dad decided to drive Ria, Andrew, Sarah, and Tyler to the amusement park as they lived nearby. Ayden and Jacob already reached there by themselves whereas Theo's elder brother dropped him off. They rode the merry-go-round, pirate ship ride, swings, and many others. They spammed their cameras with hundreds of pictures they enjoyed to the fullest. In the end, each took a candy floss and went inside the Ferris wheel. Andrew and Ria were enjoying the view, Ayden and Tyler were scared because of the height, Sarah and Theo were having a conversation for the first time and smiling whenever their eyes met, and Nina and Jacob were busy neglecting the eye contact but when Jacob said," Yes I know I have acted like a foolish asshole, I was confused about you." Nina stared at him, " No, I mean not about you I was confused about if I could be the person you deserve I still don't know about this but I can make sure I will look after you." Nina laughed and said, " what are you? My brother? Why would you look after me? The Ferris wheel stopped and everyone moved out but Jacob held Nina's hand and stopped her and they went for another round. Jacob sat beside Nina and said, "do siblings kiss?" Both laughed. "I know you need time and all sorts of thoughts must be running in your mind you can ask me all once we go back home but for now can you please hug me?" Nina never received such a proposal not only she was happy, but her eyes were also sparkling and she hugged him tightly. That hug made them realize how much they hoped well for each other. After the barbeque night, everyone went home with some wonderful memories.

Ria's eleven-eleven wishes and her prayers were finally reaching out to God. She was happy and enjoying her time with her friends.

9 Flashback

Lad selling balloons which bloom here and there
street lights were intermittent, everyone seemed unaware
cozy atmosphere build because of the bonfire
deep evocation of wandering spirits, everywhere.

Blazing stars and moon-like sun at noon
I with my friends muckrake about horror cartoon
grooming with those tunes made me swoon
hope to have a night like this soon.

Rejoicing and barbecuing was fun
windy and dark night created a commotion
sounds and strong cool winds from the ocean
through the night ends with sweet corn.

Ria wrote this amazing experience of visiting an amusement park and having dinner with her friends in her notepad and fell asleep. Sun shined, and the alarm was ringing Andrew brought coffee and she was yawning, and Ria's mother was calling her name," Ria, you are going to be late, I am leaving have your breakfast before you leave for school and take an umbrella it's raining." Ria ran downstairs and Andrew was holding an umbrella for her. Andrew never held Ria's hand in public which she wanted to but never did. While Andrew was walking on the other side of the road he grabbed Ria's waist and pulled her closer and said," still sleepy? Hold on to my hand or you may fall." Ria smiled and interlocked her hands with him. She wanted to tell him about her dreams but couldn't because she didn't know what Andrew felt about their future. So she focused on him and went to school holding hands, but as soon as she saw Ayden she ran and went towards him. Ayden watched the favorite television show Ria suggested watching. Ayden called her several times in a day for his queries and Ria helped him.

Jacob was a senior and Nina was still not ready to date him as she was expecting a clarification session. Jacob went to see Nina in her class, which made a scene because he was a basketball player and a charming senior, Nina grabbed his hand, took him near the stairs, and said," why did you come here?" "To see Ayden." Nina was confused, "What? Isn't it obvious after last night, I came to see you?" Jacob replied. Nina blushed. "Well you know seeing your face this close and the cute little things you do when you are upset, I am falling for it even more." Jacob felt shy after saying this so he faced backward and said," Here take this, I don't know if you will like it but it felt cute, yesterday near the beach a lady was selling these so I bought them but forgot to give you." It was a golden heart-shaped pendant. Nina denied taking it even though she loved it, she said, "let me first be your girlfriend then put it on me." Jacob rolled his fingers around his head and said with calmness and flirtiness," in my mind, you are already mine, baby girl," Jacob walked her to her class and took the pendant out from his wallet, and kept it silently inside Nina's pocket. Sarah was interested in Theo ever since their little conversation on the Ferris wheel but she didn't know about his sexuality so she decided to talk to Ria about it after their dance practices. While Tyler, Ayden, Samuel, and Steve were practicing their drums and guitar Gyaan walked in and asked if he could join, but everyone ignored him. Tyler felt bad for him so he went to him and said, " finally, are you guilty? There was no response and Gyaan waved his hand which meant goodbye. Ayden was playing drums and was showing off his skills, Ria and Nina were enjoying listening and vibing. Jacob and Andrew walked in together they were friends because they played football and basketball often. Nina pulled his hand and took him to the corner and said," when did you put this here? I mean thank you but you should have just put it on me, so go ahead."Jacob smiled at her and put the pendant on her. They both were finally happy together. Whereas Andrew whispered, "enjoying the time aren't you?"/Ria smiled and replied," he plays it so well, doesn't he?" "Well I can," while Andrew was speaking Ria ran toward Ayden and said, " you play it so well, can you teach me." Ayden replied with a smirk," only if you help me with Maths problems." "Deal", they both giggled they were leaving when Ria turned back and said," Simon, I will see u after school."

Rain turns its thunder and lighting into a beautiful rainbow same as the gloomy days turn into beautiful lessons. The beautiful young souls are learning and teaching each other but it is never easy.

From the deep dejection of March to jovial September, there had been many difficulties. Overcoming this the connections were sailing high even in the rain.

"Isn't it cold since last night?" Ria said. "Are you cold?" Ayden asked. "Pretty much, let's grab a coffee before we leave," Ria said. Ayden took off his layered shirt and put it on Ria. Ria laughed and said, "trying to be a gentleman?" "Weren't you cold? So take it and just drink your coffee, Ree". Ayden called Ria---Ree and Ria called Ayden----Aid, better known as First Aid, because he looked after Ria every time she needed someone his support was constant.Nina and Jacob were enjoying themselves, they played table tennis together, Jacob tried to convince Nina to play basketball but she denied saying "I am too short to aim." "Well, then I can always lift you." Nina blushed every time he flirted with her. Their friendship had turned into a beautiful romantic tale. Sarah wanted to ask Ria about Theo but she didn't because she realized she was finally happy, being with herself was the happiest time for her, grooming herself, loving herself, and being a better version of herself was the only agenda she wanted to look after at the moment. Tyler, Theo, Samuel, Steve, and Ayden worked out together after school. It started raining so they waited under the shed and chatted about some football matches after that, the guys asked each other about their current romantic status, Ayden denied saying he wasn't ready for anything yet. Samuel said he was trying to move on after seeing Sarah and Nina moving on. Steve was confused so he avoided the question as he didn't have any answers he still had feelings for Ria but couldn't do anything about it. Tyler and Theo were about to say when Ayden interrupted and said," aren't you both already dating behind our back?" Theo sighed and said," I love spending

time with Tyler but we are better off friends, what say mate?" Tyler replied, "yes, indeed."
Andrew wasn't feeling himself he was about to lose his calm because Ria wasn't giving him any attention nor was she looking after their relationship it was going on for a month according to Andrew so he decided to confront her. Ria wasn't picking up his call so he decided to check from his balcony but Ria's room lights were off so he decided to go to her place he pressed the bell but nobody answered, Andrew was anxious, when he was calling Mrs.Richards, Jacob texted him, " Bro, spend some time with me as well. I and Ayden live under the same roof, but you and Ria always visit him only." Andrew was confused so he called up Jacob first and asked "what are you talking about?" Jacob replied, " yo, weren't you here to take Ria back." Andrew asked in a zoned-out tone, "What? Ria was there?" "Well, I guess you both need some clarities, see you, tomorrow mate." Jacob hung up hastily he knew he dropped Ayden and Ria into trouble. It was raining heavily Andrew was waiting downstairs for Ria. After an hour Ayden dropped Ria at her place. Andrew in anger came there he was soaked in rainwater and asked Ria, " does it take an hour to reach home, without answering any calls?" "Bye Ree" and "Bye Aid" made the atmosphere more intense. Ria asked Andrew to continue their conversation once they get changed so Ria took Andrew to his place and offered him a towel. While Andrew was unbuttoning his shirt Ria walked in with a black t-shirt of Harry her cousin, Ria turned around Andrew was mad at her and just couldn't keep his cool. He came closer to her and said," what? do you think I am not as good as Ayden?" Ria nervously slammed the door as she was standing against

the door, Andrew was stepping closer. Earlier Ayden hugged Ria when Jacob and Nina were in the kitchen and he said," I want to be more than friends, I know you are dating Andrew and still I am being a dick." Ria stood up and shouted, "Nina. Nina. I am not feeling good can we go back home." "But it's raining, let me drop you off," Ayden said. They were stuck in traffic which took one hour to reach the home." Ria thought Jacob told Andrew what happened. Andrew said, "you know I am patient, don't you." Andrew grabbed Ria's waist held her tightly and pressed her breasts, Ria was moaning and she couldn't guess what was going on. Andrew unhooked Ria's corset top and lifted her, he wasn't kissing her so he said, "It's hard to be in this situation and not kiss you, but it's way harder to see you with another guy ho openly admires you in front of me, I guess you forgot you are mine." Ria pushed Andrew and said, "I had like to choose my peace over you both, even though our love story is not ending well it was still the best."

10 Just Us

Every time it's the day she seems to be in pain,
words that aren't comforting prick.It wasn't her fault but who to blameit's happy yet so sad it's dim but bright.

"If taking care of yourself means letting someone down, then let someone down"~Steven.

That night felt long and the pillow cover was soaked in tears, Ria was sobbing while Mr.Cuddles was barking. Andrew thought of snooping at Ria's place. So he wore his boots and with the help of his long hands and feet he successfully reached Ria's balcony. The balcony door was locked so he knocked, Ria was scared she hesitated but slightly opened the door to see who it was and Andrew held Ria's hands and walked in silence and said," be quiet, your mum will lose it if she sees me here at this time." Ria locked the doors and Andrew noticed her face was red, every time Ria cried her nose and cheeks became red, and her small Asian eyes swelled. Andrew lost it, grabbed Ria from her back, and said in frustration, anger, and tears filled in his eyes, "you will never be alone, you need my approval to end this and listen to me very carefully, this was the last time you said those words, I love you, and it's okay if you are overthinking, you feel sad, don't know the answer, need to rest today, feel insecure today, everything is fine for me just let me be by your side and love me as you do." Ria busted into tears and hugged him tightly and replied," you love me?" Andrew was shaken by her reply and said," wasn't it clear? He took a pause and while hugging her he looked into her eyes and said," well if it wasn't noticeable enough let me say it again, I have always loved you and I am loving you and will continue to love you because you make me want more." Ria had happy tears in her eyes her crying red face glowed like a blushing red face and replied," I love you so much, Simon." They both kissed each other and Ria asked him, " can you stay over until my mum wakes up?" Andrew was shocked and flustered so he asked," what are you talking about? I mean be more accurate." Ria giggled and said, " silly Simon, I want to tell you about what happened today."

Ria explained to Andrew about the evening at Ayden's place saying, " Ayden hugged me and said he likes me," Andrew interrupted and said," did he hurt you? Were you scared? I am so sorry." Ria replied," relax let me finish, I walked out of his house immediately but it was raining so he suggested that he would drop me home.

On the way, it was raining heavily and we were stuck in the traffic. I was listening to music to avoid Ayden and the scary thundering sound, he was driving roughly and was honking at people so it made it scarier. When we were about to reach he came closer and said," Ree, can we kiss once and it will be a secret." I lost it and said," if you want to see my face again stop it right now." He dropped me and I just ran towards you I was scared to death that he would cross all his limits, that's why when you tried to kiss and question me I got scared and angry and said those words. Andrew cuddled Ria and said," I am sorry and

don't worry about anything, let me take care of it." Ria said, "I can take care of it, just stay by my side."
Jacob asked Nina," so are we dating now?" Nina replied," well, we are too young to get married, so for now, yes, we are dating." They both blushed and Jacob started tickling her.

Whereas Gyaan and his new group of guilty people were regretting what they did, so they agreed to apologize to everyone the next day. Tyler and Theo were focusing on themselves and building better arms. Well, nobody can be everything to everybody so they both laughed and messed with each other all the time and everyone was in love.

It's a long day with a young feeling
relieving all those thoughts I had dear,
with whom it's worth healing.
I want back my gummy bear.

Previously it was just the way they like
lavishly I threw drama, now I know they thrive,
isn't it obvious that I am the one they dislike
and want some peace so let me just go on a drive.

Ria ended up writing all her thoughts on her notepad before going to school.

Andrew and Ria were conversing when Ayden walked into the class and said, "Ree can we talk for a moment please." Andrew replied with a sarcastic face, "In front of me." Ria asked Ayden to leave but he wanted to apologize and said," Ree you are my best friend, I couldn't control my feelings I am not asking for forgiveness just don't hate me." Ria smiled and said," "Apology not accepted also don't try to talk to me from now onwards, I will say less but I hope it's clear, isn't it?" Ayden left with a disappointed face. As soon as their conversation got over Gyaan and his guilty group Emily, Marco, Samuel, and Rowan made a circle and called Tyler, Andrew, Ria, Nina, and Ayden to apologize. Ria didn't want to hear any of their confessions so she walked out saying," I can't let my ears ache." Andrew came running to her and asked, "what's wrong?" Ria sighed and replied, "I appreciate their apology but I can never forgive them for what they did to us, I will move on but will never forget nor forgive them." Andrew smiled and replied," Do you know when I started liking you?" Ria replied," I always wanted to know but I couldn't ask." They were sitting in the corner of the classroom and Andrew whispered, " the first time I heard you play the piano, that tune I hummed every second, I thought about you, your eyes, your scent, your smile, your sensible yet bold answers for every question made me fall for you." Ria replied, " Well, it's feelings it might go away." Andrew was in shock after listening to Ria's response so he said," yes it will go away and come back stronger every time." Ria was blushing and Andrew was busy staring at her.

Theo's parents and her childhood best friend Rachel were throwing a party for him because he got selected for the Senior Football Team, Rachel had always liked Theo but he strictly believed in not dating a friend because he thought a relationship would make things complicated so he preferred friendship over the relationship. Tyler liked this thing about Theo he always appreciated it but those feelings of more than friendship were mutual but they still stayed best buddies.Nina, Jacob, Andrew, and Ria were buying gifts for Theo. Nina and Jacob left to get ready for the night whereas Ria was busy shopping for clothes and Andrew was enjoying their time together, he was just approving Ria's dresses and holding bags. They were getting ready at Ria's place and when he saw her wearing a black short dress he was too struck to speak, he just smiled and said, "you look so beautiful, my girl." Ria replied with a kiss on his neck, "and you look more handsome, Simon." They both left for the party. Everyone was enjoying the party, drinking, eating, laughing, and while dancing to slow music Andrew looked into Ria's eyes, removed her hair logs from her face, and said," Ria, You always chose peace over people but when it comes to me who will you choose?" Ria looked into Andrew's eyes and said with a smile," The moment I saw you I fell for you and I mumbled to myself,

At first, I thought it wasn't anythingbut when I stayed a little longer,it meant even more than something and I had decided I wanted to get closer.Your appearance and charm made me realizehow much power does love at first sight hold,your fragrance and voice made me mesmerizebut beauty lies in the eyes who behold.Your smile made my heart flutterI do wish to reconsider my feeling,but every time I see you my heart melts like butterand my love for you is delicate but soothing.

And so, you are my peace, Simon. I will always choose peace over people."Andrew smiled with his happy tears. Jacob, Nina, Tyler, Rachel, Andrew, Ria, Theo's classmates, and his parents made a toast for their friendship. "Cheers", and everyone was happy.

11 Family

Friendship and the bond they created in three years were just magical. In love, everything feels exciting, their presence is tempting but what happens after the heartbreak?Dos Horas- J.J Abel playing in Ria's earphones and she was writing in her notepad while waiting for Harry.

I wonder if you wish the same
didn't we deserve some more time
Like everyone says, is this the end?
No answers, because you flew away as if you had a feather.

I confessed every bit I felt, was that game?
You were the reason for my smile
Like everyone says, is this the end?
Now I have the answers because we aren't together.

Ria was at the airport waiting for Harry, they had a family dinner later that night. Mrs Richards was calling Ria to ask where was she. "I guess you are very busy looking after your new family mama, Harry is coming back today. I am at the airport waiting for him." Ria said sarcastically. Mrs Richards hung up on her. Ria and her mama have as always been supportive mother-daughter, but Ria was irritated because of so many changes in her life and it was all at once, she also noticed that all the attention and love she used to get from her mama, she had to share with her new family. She respected her mother's husband to be and he treated her like a little doll. Nathan Jones her stepdad and Otis Jones her stepbrother were a dearest family to Ria, and she was trying to get used to it. Harry's flight arrived and they tightly hugged each other and walked towards their car. Ria recently got her driver's license and she was driving the car while talking. "So what are you up to these days?" Harry asked."Stuck with some college work, driving, eating and chilling," Ria replied with a smile."Staying out to avoid your family and Andrew and chilling alone, what's wrong with you?" "Aren't there more things to worry about Harry?""Oh yeah, I forgot to ask you about your psychology studies," Harry replied eagerly."Pretty good, we are doing a campaign for mental health in three high schools this semester". "I am proud of you sister. Also, I am excited to meet my aunt, uncle and brother. Are you excited about the wedding? And I got you presents."Ria happily smiled and said," I have always wanted mama to be happy and finally she is willing to get married I am glad and excited for her.""Little sister, are you happy?" "I have a family of my own like I always wanted, yes I am on top of the world."

Nina said, "Come on Jacob, let's do this.""Are you sure?" He said."Yes, I am waiting. Should I help you?""No, I can do it. I am doing it now.""Yes, go ahead". Call going, "Guys, I am driving right now.""Just listen to what we are saying," Jacob said nervously. Nina said," We are having a sleepover this Saturday, no buts we are counting you in, you better come or I will give our matching pyjamas to

Sarah and show your drunk pictures to everyone.""Nina." And she hung up. "You better enjoy it," Harry said. Jacob asked Nina," are they coming?""Theo, Tyler, Sarah, Rachel, Holly and Andrew are coming, and I believe Ria will come too"."Is she dating anyone at the moment?" Jacob asked."I guess she is dating Archie Surfer.""Things have changed in the past year." Jacob sighed.Nina hugged him and said," Well we haven't changed, our friendship is still our priority. And it's good that they have moved on." Theo being the gamer asked,"Tyler, are you joining me tonight for the game?""I have a date, you idiot.""With whom?""With Cam Harris," Tyler replied blushing. "Enjoy, buddy." Theo sighed."Where's Rachel? Go on a date you'll are behaving like a married couple.""Whatever", Theo hung up on him.

Ria and Harry came back home, they were enjoying their dinner, and Ria was just thinking of apologizing for the whole time. Every second sitting there made her realize how her words pierced her mother's heart, she stood and hugged her mother and said, "Mumma, I am sorry if my words have hurt you, I love you and I am happy for us". Mrs Richards hugged her back and said, "no more tears you deserve only smiles. Let's make a toast to our family. Cheers."

The beautiful, positive and healthy teachings of the family make the child's life delightful, it automatically brings joy to their mind it brings peace. Still, more people and more opinions.

"I will be the light who will guide you," Andrew said to Ria.

Ria sighed and cried for an hour, she dressed up early morning and took Denver for a walk. Denver was Otis's dog and now he was like Mr. Cuddles to her.

After Theo's celebration party two years ago, Ria's dog Mr.Cuddles was diagnosed with some serious disease later that month, Mr.Cuddles died. Ria's state was miserable and after a few days, Andrew confronted her to remain, friends as they were moving to different cities and his feelings for her were changing. And later that day, Holly posted pictures of Andrew and her in a cafe. Ria wasn't ready for their breakup but he had already moved on so it was of no use she still tried to figure it out but Andrew closed all the doors on her and never opened his balcony door. Ria cried, tried to explain to him, and did all sorts of things to make their relationship work, he didn't even give a valid reason for their breakup so she assumed he had lost interest in her and all he did was reply to her texts very often as if nothing ever happened.

It went like that for straight two months and finally, Ria left for her college. While recalling her breakup, Ria was playing Faded- Alan Walker on her piano and her tears dropped off her chin she sobbed but continued playing. Theo rang the doorbell, and Otis somehow managed to open the door. Theo brought the confectionaries for him and knocked at Ria's room," I am coming in".Ria was crying, Theo ran to her and hugged her. "I miss him, I miss him like crazy. Even though his sense of humor is worse, he ditched me but his presence gave me assurance and comfort.""Ria, calm down. He is a jerk he broke up with you and now he is enjoying with that girl Holly. You should focus on the person who loves you. And he is Archie, not Andrew.""But, Andrew loved me.""Yes, loved.

He will never realize how much a girl ever loved him or maybe he will after Holly dumps him."
They tightly hugged each other and discussed what is wrong at the moment.

Otis Jones knocked at Ria's room he is twelve years younger than her. Ria gave her room to him and she shifted to the guest room. She answered the door and said," Do you need something Ooty?""Sister, can you help me with my homework.""Yes, why not. Come in.""Sister.""Yes, Ooty.""Is he your boyfriend?Am I not your brother?""Who said that? You are my dearest little brother, come to me or just call me if anything goes wrong, alright? This is Uncle Theo, Sister's best friend like you are my best friend.""Uncle? Otis, she is not your sister Ria, she is Aunt Ria.Otis gave a heartwarming smile to Ria, and all three were laughing at each other.
Later, that day it was a Friday gaming night at Jacob's house. "Hey Andrew, how are you doing?" Nina asked."Better, how are you?" Andrew replied."Good to know, I am doing perfectly alright touch wood." Andrew nervously asked, "Any news from Ria? How's her college? Did she find someone new, I haven't seen her since that day?"Nina replied, "Ever since you moved to another city, Ria, Theo and Rachel and their new friend Archie Surfer is chilling together the whole day. Whenever he is around he makes sure Ria laughs. They hung out the entire summer. Archie has a soft corner for her, but he knew that she still wasn't over his ex-boyfriend. So he took a step back, but one day on the subway, he was sitting beside Ria. Ria always wears a visually impaired watch, so he asked her why she wore it. She simply said," it

makes me realize how important every second is. Thanks for asking nobody noticed it ever."Archie replied," like you haven't noticed my feelings ever."A little kid was running around so he offered his seat to him. Ria smiled at him, it was raining heavily, and Archie was holding groceries and on the other hand, he was holding an umbrella. Ria went back to her memory when you were protecting her from getting soaked in rain. Ria held Archies hand and said," can you kiss me?" Archie dropped the umbrella and groceries and kissed Ria. "Ria, I am afraid to lose you and you are not even mine.""I don't want to listen anymore, Nina. I see they are really happy together."

"Yes, they are happy together, at least that's what it looks like."

"Good to know, are they coming tomorrow?""Only Ria will be coming, where is Holly though?""She is on her menstrual cycle, so she couldn't make it". " Fine, you talk to the boys. I will go get some snacks"Andrew sighed and took a sip of beer.

13 Te Odio. Te Amo.

She stammers, bites her lips, shakes her legs
her eyes twitch, and the nervousness in her begs.
The beautiful words that I hold in my hand and tongue
I write it all down, it does make me slight fatigue.
She has been happier and merrier, thanks to the fortune she holds.
But the thought of the upcoming future makes her fold.
The strength and pleasure which she receives are from herself then I deliver those gifts to oneself.

Ria felt miserable in the past few days, she avoided Andrew and Archie. She wanted to be sure of her choices and priorities, so she took Nathan's advice and stayed indoors to practice some songs and was attending some online classes for her psychology campaign which helped her think it through.Her friends tried to figure out the situation and help her, but things weren't even in their favor. She decided to face the situation herself in a few days.

Nina asked Jacob to come over for a meal and she wanted to ask what was going on between them. Jacob arrived straight and went to Nina's room, he didn't even knock. Nina was dressing up, he came closer to her and gave her a tight back hug. Nina was startled," Gosh, you scared me." "Just stay like this for a few minutes, I know I screwed up. I was being an asshole.""Absolutely.""Can you give me another chance?""If you would like to explain.""It was our first time, we were both more or less drunk. I don't remember much, I thought you hated me and you didn't like it."Nina giggled and tried to control her laugh."What? Are you laughing?"Nina made eye contact with Jacob and smiled at him."You don't remember? Then I shall make sure you remember from now on. Nina slowly kissed him, and Jacob build the intensity of their kiss. Jacob carried her in his arms and Nina whispered, "I want to do it near the mirror, I don't want you to miss out on anything.""As you please, babe."He carried her and pinned her against the mirror. They were kissing each other, he started kissing her neck and he bent slowly and kissed her thighs, he licked between her legs, while she was moaning and smiling. He slipped his middle finger inside her, she was moaning his name and he whispered, "I barely started babe.""Be quiet, and continue."Nina had already wet, and her elder sister knocked in and said, "you two come out, everyone is waiting for you for dinner." "Gosh, we are coming.""We can continue at my place after dinner, babe."They both smiled, cleaned themselves, and went downstairs.

Theo called Sarah, "We need to talk, can we meet at the Cafe in an hour?""Sure."Theo was already there, he came half an hour before. Sarah arrived and sat beside her, he stood and sat across the table. "Are you here to reject me?""Who am I to reject you? You are a wonderful human, it's just that I have feelings for someone else.""I know it's Tyler. It's okay, I didn't wish or hoped for any commitments, I just wanted to confess and give us a try. I wanted to tell you, show you, and make you feel the way I feel for you. I have always liked you and I don't know if I can move on easily. But I wish you and Tyler the very best future ahead. Also, it's your loss.""Completely, I am sad for letting you go. But we still are friends?" "We can't be friends, Theo. It's never that simple. But yes hit me up, if you ever get heartbroken, not that I wish for it, just saying.""I promise I will."They hugged each other and went down their respective paths. Later, Theo texted Rachel saying,"We should part our ways."And she replied, "Ok."

Theo wanted to fix everything at once so he asked Tyler to meet him at 11/4 Bar because the bar is a place where the lights are dim and we have to come close to hear each other because it's crowded. Their legs go around yours when your stools face each other. Different cocktails and mocktails, make one a little tipsy, giggles and eye contact make it convenient for a confession. But it isn't as easy as it sounds.

They don't regret it.They knew it would hurt them and they did it anyway. They are sad but at least they got to learn a lot. It wasn't only Sarah but it was Rachel, Theo, Andrew, and Ria. They were all going through a rough phase called heartbreak season.

The other night, Tyler didn't show up at the bar. Theo waited for three hours. Well, Theo wasn't upset about waiting for him because Tyler waited for him for so many years. And Theo realized he didn't love him, he just loved the attention and friendship he shared with Tyler. Even though he was hurt, he realized it is better to have friendships rather than a relationship.Later Tyler sent him a voice note in the morning saying, "Hey, sorry. Did you wait long? I didn't mean to be a jerk but I was stuck with Cam, we crashed at his place last night. We did it and I think I like him more now."In response to this, Theo said, "No problem, we can talk later, it wasn't necessary. By the way, I am happy for you."Theo was feeling depressed and hopeless, he needed Ria but she was stuck with her problems, so he realized Sarah could be a good listener and a great advisor. He called her and within a few moments she showed up at his place. Theo was nervous to say a word, after a silence of straight ten minutes. She finally said,

" I knew that you weren't for me, but deep down I wanted you to be."

This is exactly how we are feeling, isn't it?Theo was about to cry and Sarah stood up and sat beside him. She patted him and Theo hugged her tightly. "You said you didn't want me to get any wrong idea nor get my hopes high."Theo said," Can you help me forget him?""I can at least try but using me for moving on, I don't think it's a good idea. But I want to do it anyway."Theo looked into Sarah's eyes, he heldher hands and pulled her closer, he interlocked her hands with his hands and kissed her. "It wasn't our first kiss," she said."Though it felt like that."They continued making out.

Ria was busy preparing for the wedding of her mother and Nathan Jones. Archie came to help her with the preparations. He surprised her early morning with the help of Ms. Richards. Ria was happy to see him but he had several questions around him.While they were normally having a conversation, Archie asked, "Is everything alright?" "Yes, why? Do I look weird?""You look beautiful. I meant is everything alright between us? You hardly replied to my texts, you didn't call me ever since you came here.""We will talk later about it, you must be tired. You can take a nap in my room.I am taking Denver for a walk."Archie knew something was wrong but held his temper and didn't show any tantrums because it was a very important occasion for her. "Are you not even going to hug me."Ria hugged him, Archie tightly hugged her and said," I missed you and I miss us. Let's go back as soon as we are done here.""Sure. By the way, are you growing your facial hair?""Is it weird?""No, it suits you. Even I missed you."Archie gave a peck on her forehead and Ria smiled at him but within, her heart was breaking. She cheated on him with her ex-boyfriend which is the worst of all and the fact that she never loved him.

This weekend the wedding was at St.Teresa Church and the gathering was at their new house at night. All her friends were coming over to the gathering but the wedding was to be attended by the family members. Ria and Ms. Olivia, Ms. Richards's best friends were the bridesmaids. Ria was very excited and happy. Harry and her rest six male cousins arrived a day before. Ria's Grandpa was getting emotional every other second because he always wanted her daughter to get married again and finally his dream was coming true. Ria was finally having a family of her own, which made her emotional but she wanted everybody's day to be special, so she had planned a musical at the gathering later.

14 Wedding

While love was at someone's door, the harsh reality was hitting the spot.

Tyler always wanted to do something of his own, he was just twenty-one, and he started trading to be on his own feet.Ria was already earning through her psychology campaigns, he was inspired by her but also envied her. Theo was graduating from business studies as he wished to join his family business of Bush Textiles.Nina and Jacob were graduating from a law university. Jacob's parents wanted him to study management but he chose his preference over his parents. He didn't choose to disrespect him but he did choose it for his happiness. Instead of Jacob, Ayden went to study Management in London.Andrew always worshipped music, but he chose music as his part-time passion and is now studying Engineering as his main course.Ria, Archie, Theo, Nina, and Jacob met often even though they were busy with their college.

Theo called up Ria to explain to her what is happening with him in the past two days.Ria replied to it by saying,"remove some people from your life, be more particular about your priorities and all your problems will no longer be a problem for you. The sooner you chose peace over people everything will turn in your favor. Also, you owe a sincere apology to Rachel.*Theo replied," Yes, you are right. And I am sorry for that day, I shouldn't have lost my temper.""You just said the truth.I am going to the church later, confessing my sin will not gonna compensate for my infidelity but maybe Jesus could forgive me."Theo was confused about what he liked, and whom he liked. Sarah wasn't being a busy body she just lived in the moment, she was just happy for the fact that Theo at least thinks of her and maybe this could be more than just friends with benefits.

The wedding was on the head, preparations were going well.Finally, on Wednesday, it was the wedding day.
"Yes, it's happening. After dating for two years, finally, they have tied the knot."
"They are officially pronounced man and wife."Ria's grandpa Ross, Ms. Olivia, and Ria we're getting emotional. Archie stood beside Ria and held her hands tightly, joy and love were in the air. After the pictures session, there was a feast waiting for dinner.
When they went back to their new home, Nina arranged everything as Ria planned. The dinner was on the backyard lawn it was filled with continental dishes, and the house was filled with candles, fairy lights, rose petals, and apple scent.The food looked appetizing.Everyone had a huge smile on their faces.And the musical was about to begin.Ria started playing the Piano. Nina, Tyler, Theo, and Sarah were singing 'A thousand Years' by Christina Perri.Everyone was enjoying the music and food.There was a dance to end the perfect day.Mr. Jones and Mrs. Jones started the dance to the music 'The Night We Met'

by Lord Huron.The music Andrew and Ria danced to at Theo's party two years ago.Ria left the lawn and ran inside, followed by Archie."Ria, wait. We should dance.""I am not feeling good. I need some air.""It's just one song.""Archie, please.,"Archie pulled her hand and tried to convince her."She said she didn't want to", Andrew yelled.

"It is like that sometimes isn't it?What you want is exactly in not your favor. It's been a few days since I have been feeling the darkest but it's still alright as long as I have the possibility of getting stronger and stronger.Some people are dealing with some actual problems in their life, people are losing their loved ones, a few are battling against disease and poverty, and the women and children are enduring suffocations from society and the brutal truth of life. And here I am doing absolutely nothing, being sad for some guys who don't deserve to ruin my mental peace. Now that everything is revealed, Mom is married, it's now time for a comeback. Peace over People is sailing."Ria wrote this on her notepad and packed her bags. She decided to go back to her college and start preparing for her psychology campaigns.

She loved you for four summers and three winters.She tried and is trying but couldn't move on.The day she thought she had no feelings left she packed her bags and tried to leave.

"Nathan, you wake up this early? It's five in the morning.""Well, I should have asked that question. What are these suitcases? Are you going somewhere?""I am going back to college.""Without even seeing off your mother?""I left a note and yes, please look after Mumma and Otis like you do, and thanks for everything.,"Nathan patted Ria's head and said," Before you go just check that box in the hall drawer. There's a package for you, it was with the watchman."He pointed towards the drawer.Ria opened the box it was a visually impaired watch and there was a note.

"Asshole," Ria muttered.

"Thanks, Nathan. I will come back soon.""We will be waiting. Take care, dear."Ria hugged Nathan and she left for the airport.

"My love was pure
but it wasn't sufficient
you only gave me lies
but I kept the promises alive
I held your hand even
in the worst time
but you left when it was perfect and fine."

15 Amor Fati

It's not a fairy tale nor a Netflix rom-com movie where two strangers meet, fall in love and then face a problem and then reconcile and live happily ever after. What an absolute fuck?I haven't met someone in a subway, library, airport, grocery store, or a suicidal spot where do we find such people, how do they fall in love at first sight?"

"Breathe in, breathe out. You are doing great, and so what positive things are you thinking of right now?"
"Positive things? Miss Lana, umm, it's nothing just thinking about what should I eat while watching Jujutsu Kaisen".
"Ugh, I can't help you, dear."Cell phone ringing, "Theo I told you, it's not meant for me. Miss Lana told me not to come for yoga classes from tomorrow as if I desperately go there every morning".
"It would only help you," Sarah said."What are you two doing together early morning?"Theo moaned," Sarah.""Jesus Christ, you both are gross."Sarah interrupted and said," Are you done packing? We are leaving tomorrow morning."
"I don't understand why is it like that. We go on a vacation for our summer and fall for someone, do mediocre and romantic stuff together, and have a happy ending, and what happens after that?Do they meet again? Do they live

happily ever after?I am not an anti-romance kinda person nor I am going through the anti-love syndrome, does it make sense? It's just that I didn't have any meet-cute nor any proposal ever since I broke up with the two guys. My dog Denver's life is more interesting than mine."
"So finally you have realized you are missing out on your fun, well better late than never. Avoid your psychology studies for the time being and focus on your love life. Make love and have fun on this vacation.""With you couples? I will be doomed."
Ria sighs and ends the phone call.While having lunch in a Japanese restaurant, Ria mutters to herself,"I enjoy my company, slurping coffee three times a day, work and work it is my lifestyle now and I enjoy it because everything I do seems to be in the loop, but at least I have peace. But my heart is bored of the peace.It's been a year and I want to create a better future so that I don't regret it.It will be fine I guess, maybe waiting is better and someone good for me shall come to me, maybe on the trip."Ria texts on the group chat.

I felt miserable today I don't hate my life
Just the phase I blame
I do wanna cry but it doesn't
make me feel better in any possible way.
Yes, of course, I know
many face more problems than I do
my smile and my tears don't concern anyone,
the goodbyes, and welcomes I miss
but what should I do right now?

Ria ate sushi for her dinner and drove straight to the mall, she shopped for her trip which was tomorrow. Ria broke up with Archie and also she cut her ties with Andrew after a massive argument between all three of them, Ria apologized to Archie for cheating and said,"fucking Andrew was a mistake and a huge regret."Andrew in anger said,"I feel the same way."

And it's been more than a year since their fight.Nobody ever contacted each other, three of them went on their respective path and they realized, how "Peace over People rules and sails".